A
NEW MEXICO
PRIMER

For Students of All Ages

A
NEW MEXICO PRIMER

For Students of All Ages

R. Kermit Hill, Jr.

SANTA FE

© 2011 by R. Kermit Hill, Jr.
All Rights Reserved.

No part of this book may be reproduced in any form or by any electronic or mechanical means including information storage and retrieval systems without permission in writing from the publisher, except by a reviewer who may quote brief passages in a review.

Sunstone books may be purchased for educational, business, or sales promotional use. For information please write: Special Markets Department, Sunstone Press, P.O. Box 2321, Santa Fe, New Mexico 87504-2321.

Book and Cover design • Vicki Ahl
Body typeface • Franklin Gothic Book
Printed on acid free paper

Library of Congress Cataloging-in-Publication Data

Hill, R. Kermit, 1942-
 A New Mexico primer : for students of all ages / by R. Kermit Hill, Jr.
    p. cm.
 ISBN 978-0-86534-797-7 (softcover : alk. paper)
 1. New Mexico--History. 2. New Mexico--History--Study and teaching. I. Title.
 F796.H64 2011
 978.9--dc22
                        2010052681

WWW.SUNSTONEPRESS.COM
SUNSTONE PRESS / POST OFFICE BOX 2321 / SANTA FE, NM 87504-2321 /USA
(505) 988-4418 / ORDERS ONLY (800) 243-5644 / FAX (505) 988-1025

Starvation Peak towers above the village of Tecolote near Las Vegas. Illustration from *Guide to the Pacific Coast* by C. A. Higgins, 1896.

An early illustration of El Morro (Inscription Rock), now a National Monument, has the signature of Don Juan de Oñate in 1605. From *Marvels of the New West* by William Thayer, 1888.

Contents

Introduction ____9

1 In the Beginning ____11

2 Old Spain ____17

3 Revolutions ____23

4 War Most Uncivil ____29

5 The Wild West ____33

6 Unforeseen Change ____41

7 On the World Stage ____47

8 The New World ____51

Timeline ____55

Guide For Teachers ____57

Glossary ____59

Author's Suggested New Mexico Reading List ____64

Fifty-Plus Books on New Mexico from Sunstone Press____67

Emigrants stopping for supplies along the Santa Fe Trail. Illustration from *Harper's*, July, 1880.

Introduction

New Mexico has a delightfully interesting history. I learned it from living here, traveling, reading, and teaching for 43 years. This little work is an appetizer for newcomers and a reminder for the initiated. There is a recommended reading list at book's end. It is just the beginning of a long trip. Have fun.

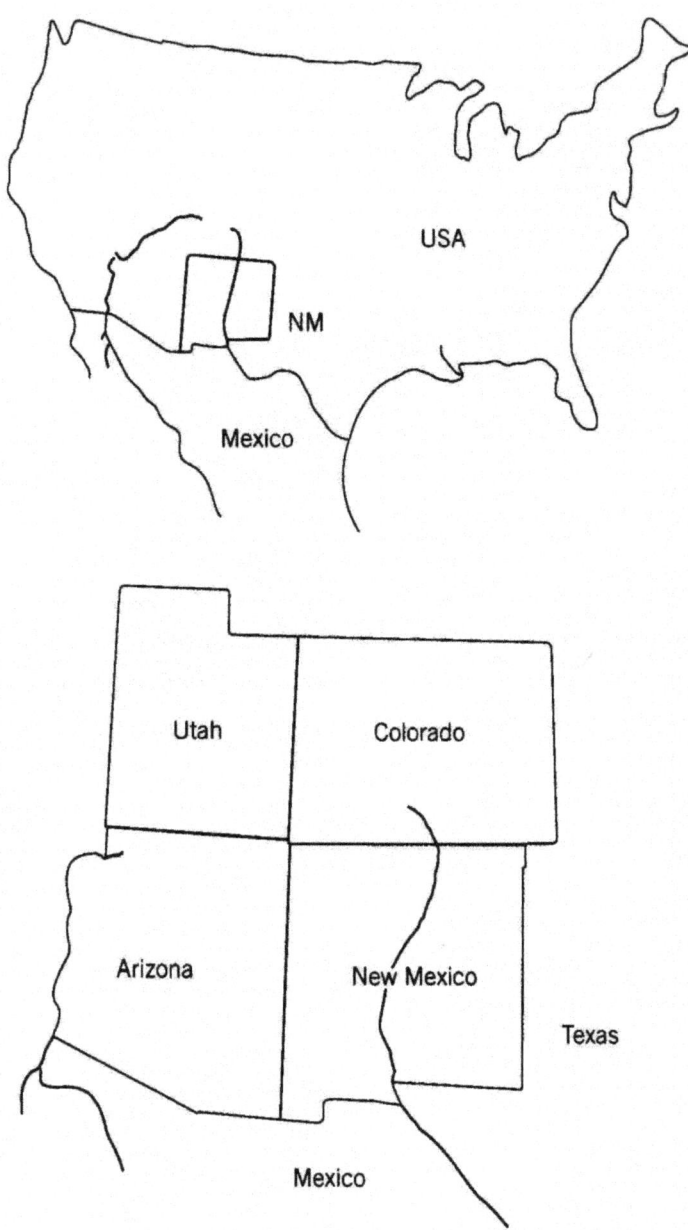

NEW MEXICO IN THE UNITED STATES

1

In the Beginning

In the Miocene, Pleistocene, Oligocene and other scenes the oceans laid down beds of limestone and sandstone. Large reptiles roamed the land that began to form. Meteors hit, volcanoes erupted, earthquakes occurred, and the dinosaurs became oil. The earth moved about, pushing up mountains here, breaking them off there, and all the while rain and wind eroded them. Seas receded, icecaps formed, and melted. New Mexico had everything from glaciers to rain forests. Today it is mostly desert with less surface water than any other state.

It eventually lost touch with the sea coast by 600 miles in any direction. The various kinds of mountains it developed cut off moisture-laden breezes, creating rain shadows, otherwise known as deserts. The mountains also collected snow and rain, which ran downhill creating rivers, which ironically run through some of the driest deserts.

A while after the last ice age a few humans wandered into New Mexico from the north. They were culinary tourists, looking for food in the form of prairie dogs, giant bison, woolly mammoths, camels and horses—which they ate, not rode. They killed these animals with spears tipped with beautiful flint heads called Folsom points. They camped at Folsom, Clovis, in the Sandias, and other places. For reasons we can only guess, the animals died out and the early humans either died or went home.

Because this will become an issue later, we must note that these guys were not necessarily Indians, just humans. Eventually more humans came through the northwest from the Far East—that is, Asia—and by about 5000 years ago they were what would later be called *Indians*.

They, too, roamed around hunting animals, piñons, prickly pear fruit and shelter. They liked caves, if any were to be had. Otherwise they dug holes and covered them with branches. They had fire, so living where wood was available was good. That was in the more mountainous regions of New Mexico. Somewhere along the way some of them domesticated corn, beans, squash and chile, plus a few turkeys. Thus was born New Mexican food.

To raise these crops they had to stay put. They learned to build with rock and trees. A thousand or so years ago the Chaco Culture of the San Juan Basin was a result of this knowledge. Like all humans they overdid it. They used up resources, fought over them, watched the climate change, and finally had to move again. This happened several times. By the 1300s the Chaco people were living near the Rio Grande, still farming and building villages.

It should be no surprise that these people worshipped the sun, the rain and the animals which fed them. Their lives were generally short and uncertain. There were never very many of them, relatively speaking. Then their problems got worse. New nomadic hunters appeared from the north who attacked them. The newcomers were initially Athapascans, known later as Apaches and Navajos. Uto Shoshonean peoples also appeared. The Navajo named the ancient pueblo dwellers whose ruined villages they saw *Anasazi*—our ancient enemy. The Navajo called themselves *The People*. They were human after all, and quite capable of labeling others who were different.

This is a good time to point out that each group/tribe was a different ethnic group, speaking a different language or dialect and following different customs. They were as diverse as Europeans, Africans and Asians. We speak of *Pueblo* or *nomads* referring to a style of life, not a language group.

From the 1300s to the 1500s these stone-age peoples merrily battled for control of New Mexico's limited resources, using their stone weapons and tools.

Pueblo Indian community house, Taos. Illustration from *Illustrated New Mexico, 1885, Fifth Edition*, by W. G. Ritch.

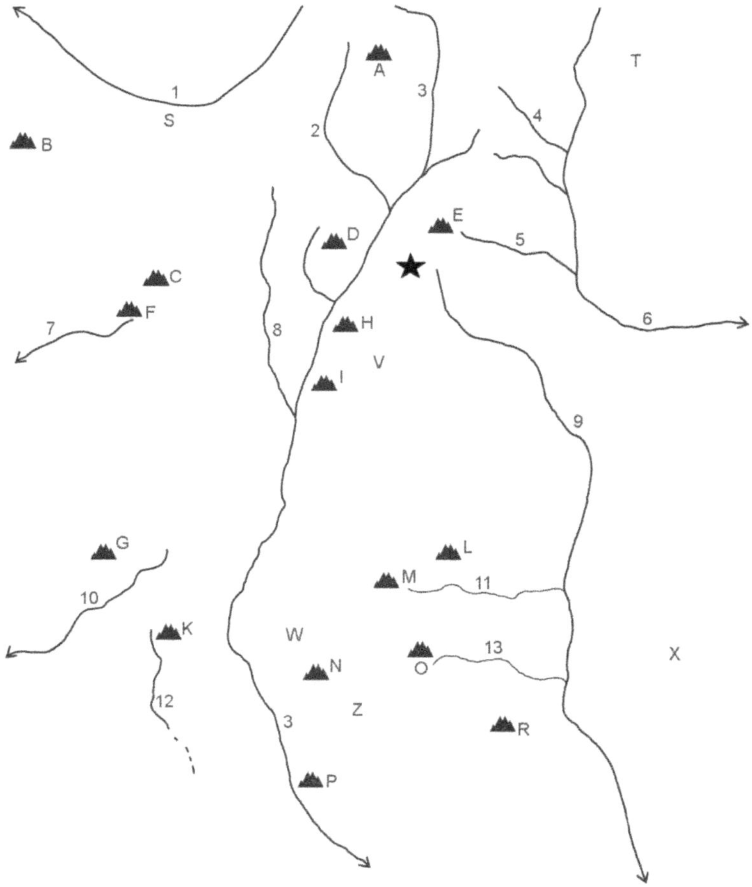

1. San Juan River
2. Chama River
3. Rio Grande
4. Cimarron River
5. Mora River
6. Canadian River
7. Zuni River
8. Rio Puerco
9. Pecos River
10. Gila River
11. Rio Hondo
12. Mimbres River
13. Rio Penasco

A. San Juan
B. Chuska
C. Mt. Taylor
D. Jemez
E. Sangre De Cristo
F. Zuni
G. Mogollon
H. Sandia
I. Monzano

K. Black Range
L. Capitan
M. Sierra Blanca
N. San Andres
O. Sacramento
P. Organ
R. Guadalupe

S. San Juan Basin
T. Raton Plateau
V. Estancia Valley
W. Jornada del Muerto
X. Llano Estacado
Z. Tularosa Basin

PHYSICAL FEATURES OF NEW MEXICO

★ Modern Santa Fe
Current Boundaries Did Not Exist Before 1850

Mountains ▲   Rivers ⌒

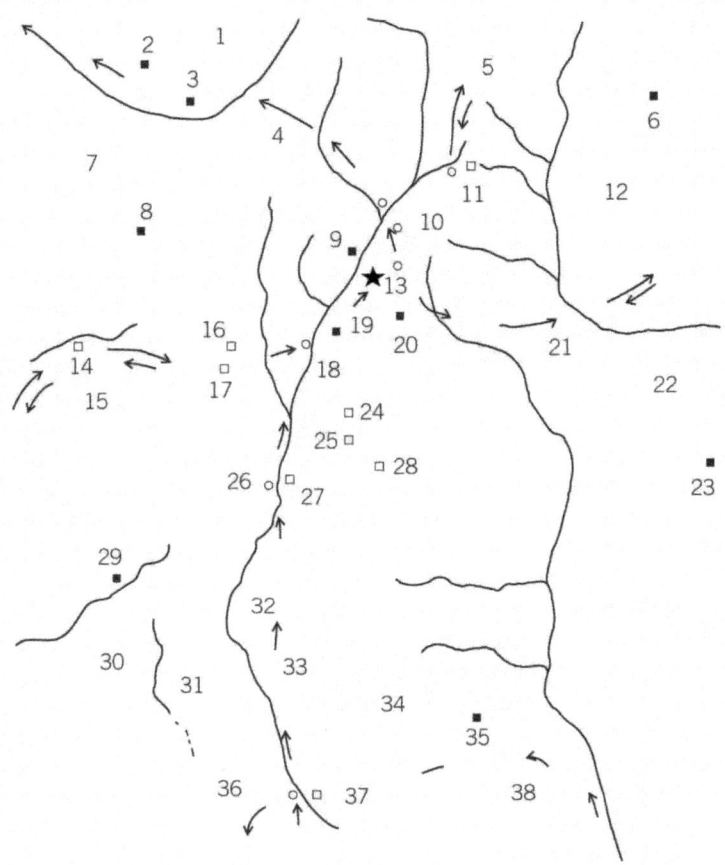

1. Ute	12. Jicarilla Apaches	23. Clovis
2. Mesa Verde	13. Santa Fe ★	24. Quarai
3. Aztec	14. Zuni	25. Abo
4. Escalante	15. Coronado	26. Socorro
5. De Anza	16. Laguna	27. Piros
6. Folsom	17. Acoma	28. Gran Quivera
7. Navajo	18. Albuquerque	29. Gila
8. Chaco Canyon	19. Sandia	30. Western Apache
9. Frijoles	20. Galisteo	31. Mimbres
10. Santa Cruz	21. Coronado	32. Onate
11. Taos	22. Comanche	

ANCIENT, PRE-SPANISH AND NOMADIC INDIANS IN SPANISH NEW MEXICO

Spanish New Mexico ○   Pueblos Ca. 1600 ▫   Ancient Peoples Sites ■
Spanish Explorers   ⟶

2

Old Spain

Meanwhile, over in Europe and Africa people were moving around fighting each other, too. Resources were an issue, but their disagreements over who was the central figure of their religions was an even greater one. They fought almost constantly over this. In Spain the war went on for over 700 years between Christians and Moslems. Sometimes it was just between Christians and Christians. An Italian fellow named Polo went to China where he found desirable items which Europeans considered luxuries—and wanted. Because the Moslems controlled much of this trade, Spain, two centuries later, sent another Italian looking for a safer route to the goodies of China. He was lost, bumped into America, and Spain claimed the place. Soon they were exploring everywhere in the newfound world where they hoped to find gold to pay for those goodies and to attain power. In 1539 one of them named *Head of a Cow* visited New Mexico while on tour. He heard there was gold there.

So Francisco Coronado came north from Old Mexico to find a New Mexico. He stayed two years, 1540-1542, found no gold, irritated the natives, and went home. Others followed in the next 60 years—they just could not believe there was no gold in the north after all the wealth found in Mexico and Peru.

Spain also had religious issues. The rulers wanted everyone to be a Roman Catholic Christian. At the moment in history when Spain found the New World, it also chose to expel all the Jews and Moslems from Spain. Many Jews came to America to escape persecution. Spain wanted to rule Europe and the China trade. Germans, Englishmen and Dutchmen were offended so they revolted. They created their own churches and long, bloody wars ensued. In 1588-1589 Spain attempted to attack England and was severely defeated by weather, poor leadership and the English. Spain arced into decline. Santa Fe did not exist yet.

In 1598 Juan de Oñate brought a colony of Spaniards, some perhaps Jewish, to New Mexico. They settled near Española. He began a policy of forcing Indians to become Christians, partly to offset the losses of north European protestors. He had the technological advantage of guns, iron swords, armor and horses, coupled with a deep belief in his cause. The natives may not have been happy with Oñate, but they wanted these tools and animals, too, and they could not make them. They either had to buy or steal them. The nomadic tribes were quite adept at the latter and soon they were even more nomadic, and dangerous.

The pueblos had no gold. Soon Spain gave up on the idea. New Mexico would be a buffer to protect the rich silver mines of Mexico. The colony was ruled strictly by Spain yet left much on its own. The Church and constantly-rotating governors fought over power. The Spanish, Pueblos and nomads were always in a low-grade war. Spain tried to hold New Mexico with less than 200 soldiers. The colony was isolated by distance and a deadly desert.

The Spanish assumed that their safety lay in all worshipping their God. The Indians felt pretty much the same way. Conflict was bound to happen. It came to a head in 1680 when an Indian named Popé, whom the Spanish had severely punished, led a revolt. He united all the tribes, who killed many Spaniards and chased the rest out to El Paso del Norte. Popé then got the big head and lost control of the diverse tribes of his alliance.

England and France were firmly planted in America by 1690, creating a threat to Spanish hegemony. Spain sent Don Diego de Vargas north in 1692–1693. The technological advantage and the disarray of the Indians led to a relatively bloodless re-conquest still celebrated today through the Santa Fe Fiesta. The Spaniards and Pueblos settled on a *live and let live* policy, allying them against the Apaches, Navajos, Utes and Comanches.

In 1715, Spain withdrew its military border far to the south. New Mexico entered a somnolent period as a forgotten outpost of a declining empire. Its people dug *acequias* along the mountain streams flowing to the Rio Grande, built a new town of Albuquerque (now called Old Town), raised sheep, goats, cattle and horses, hunted, fought the nomads and lost touch with the world, which was rapidly changing.

Once a year an oxcart caravan struggled to bring in limited goods in exchange for the limited supplies of wool and hides the colony had. Spain governed from Spain, and it took a year on average for a message to circulate from Santa Fe to Sevilla and back via Mexico City.

In the 1760s there was a brief renaissance in Spain and Mexico when a French King took the throne. Many Spaniards then realized how far behind northern Europe they had fallen. Besides, Russia was in Alaska. A string of missions were established up the California coast. De Anza became governor of New Mexico. He sent an expedition to California to try to establish a trade route, which did not ultimately happen. He did defeat the Comanches in Colorado, signaling to the French to back off. He, too, left New Mexico and it fell back into its torpor. The great smallpox epidemic of the 1700s killed thousands of New Mexicans.

But, a new nation was aborning on the Atlantic Coast. It was English, Protestant, a full heir to the Enlightenment and Industrial Revolutions, and it was going dynamic. In 1790 there were 25,000 Spanish and Pueblo people in New Mexico. There were 3.5 million English and African people in the U.S., aimed west. France revolted, too, drawing Spain into the fray with all of Europe. Ideas of independence, freedom, and equality could not be quarantined. They infected Mexico.

The dynamic new kid on the block, the United States of America, bought the Louisiana Purchase in 1803 and sent Lieutenant Zebulon Pike to explore the southern part of it. He got himself captured by Spanish troops and became a tourist in Santa Fe. He was released and promptly reported to the U.S. about a people hungry for modern things.

Evidence of New Mexico's isolation appeared around 1800. The Church in Mexico had largely abandoned the province, so the people took on their own spiritual needs by promoting chapters of the Third Order of St. Francis, known popularly as *Penitentes*. These fraternities filled in many functions the Church was not present to administer and more firmly bonded the community. The movement was medieval in origin and tone, and would later be the source of much controversy. It also held a dark fascination for outsiders. The *Penitentes* and Pike perhaps symbolize two polar opposites coming into conflict.

**Lieutenant Zebulon Pike.
Illustration from *Massacres of the Mountains* by J. P. Dunn Jr., 1886.**

Procession of Penitentes at San Antonito, a small village in the Sandias. Illustration from *Harper's Weekly*, September 7, 1889.

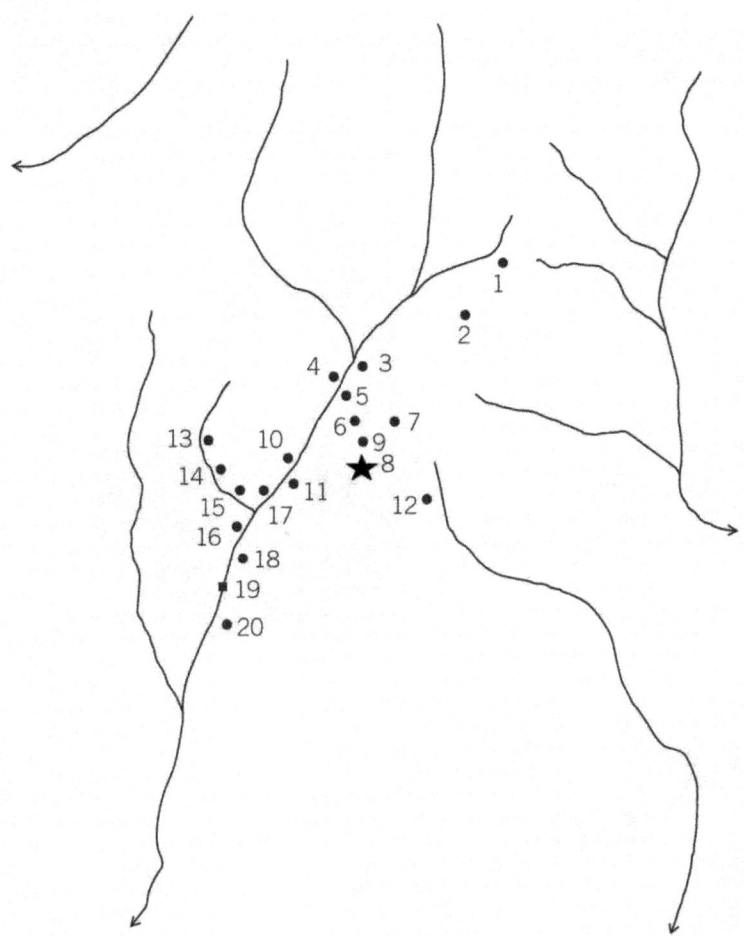

1. Taos
2. Picuris
3. San Juan (Ohkay Owingeh)
4. Santa Clara
5. San Idelfonso
6. Pojoaque
7. Nambe
8. Santa Fe ★
9. Tesuque
10. Cochiti
11. Santo Domingo (Kewa)
12. San Felipe
13. Pecos
14. Jemez
15. Zia
16. Santa Ana
17. Tiguex
18. Sandia
19. Albuquerque
20. Isleta

NORTHERN RIO GRANDE PUEBLOS

3

Revolutions

Between 1810 and 1821 Mexico revolted. As soon as it was independent, Mexico opened its borders to trade with the U.S., and New Mexico became part of the United States. Many will argue this point, but it is true. William Becknell drove a wagon load of goodies to Santa Fe; the people loved them and were thereafter attached to the U.S. They certainly were not Mexicans in a true sense—in fact, they were entering a long period of identity crisis.

The Santa Fe Trail had been born. Every year it brought more goods and people of diverse ethnicity. The Spanish-speakers labeled them all *Anglos* because they spoke mostly English. Some belonged to the Anglican Church. Some New Mexicans joined the trade, opening their world view.

Fur trappers came to the mountains looking for beaver. Taos became a major center of that trade from 1821 to 1840. It included a number of Frenchmen and one of the most famous of all western characters, Kit Carson.

Mexico remained very unstable, suffering 48 governments in 25 years, many of them military dictatorships. New Mexicans felt ignored and believed they could better govern themselves. In 1837 they killed a Mexican governor. The most famous figure of this period was Manuel Armijo, who served as governor several times. In 1836 Texas revolted, declared independence, and New Mexico faced a new threat. Texas claimed the entire Rio Grande as its western border. In 1841 they tried to claim it by invasion, only to be defeated by geography—they got lost looking for the square. Armijo captured them and, through his own brutality, damaged relations further. The *Tejanos* were persistent critters.

New Mexico expanded a little under Mexican rule. Spain had granted land ownership to the Pueblos and to Spanish communities. This land was to be used communally. These grants lay along the Rio Grande, from the El Paso area to Taos. Mexico gave out more grants, spreading fan-like along the upper Pecos, the Cimarron, Mora, Chama and Rio Grande valleys. These grants included both communal lands and land given specifically to individuals in sizes much larger than the Spanish grants. This expansion was in part a belated effort to forestall the rapidly expanding United States. These grants have been a source of controversy ever since.

Anglo merchants established trade centers in the 1830-40s at the main towns along the Rio Grande. *Anglo* is used loosely here since some of them were of French origin, others Germans and

Jewish, and some were Scots or Scotch-Irish. They sent Mexican silver and mules plus beaver pelts back to Missouri in exchange for metal tools, textiles, ceramics and weapons made in U.S. and European factories.

By the 1840s many Americans had decided that the U.S. was destined by fate to control all—or most of—North America, an attitude not at all unusual among humans. In 1845 a decision was made to annex Texas, which led to war with Mexico. In two years the U.S. defeated Mexico, forcing it to cede a large territory, mostly empty of Mexicans, to the U.S. This territory was divided into California, Utah and New Mexico.

New Mexico was taken by an army commanded by General Stephen W. Kearney in 1846. Manuel Armijo, faced with superior technology and organization, chose not to fight. Kearney marched on to California. In 1847 a group of Taos Indians and some Spanish New Mexicans revolted against the new government, killing Governor Charles Bent in Taos. The U.S. suppressed the revolt. Blame was attached in part, if unfairly, to Father Martinez of Taos. He was a New Mexican patriot and probably felt some fear that this new Protestant people would attack the Catholic Church.

In the period 1846–1850, Mormons established Utah, gold was discovered in California, Irishmen and Germans flooded into America, and the slavery controversy approached a crisis. The Great Compromise of 1850 settled a border between New Mexico and Texas. New Mexico began to look like New Mexico. In 1853 the southwest corner of New Mexico was added by another treaty with Mexico. Texas was allowed to have slavery. The Territory of New Mexico could choose to have or not have slavery. In the next ten years they voted three times — no, yes, no. The Territory was becoming divided. More Texans moved in to southern New Mexico. Many of the Spanish upper class held Indian slaves already, so they were conflicted. The north was tied to New England commercially. In Arizona a different population was developing, which led to creation of a separate territory in 1863.

General Stephen Watson Kearney's troops crossing New Mexico Mountains. Illustration from *Harper's Magazine*, 1880.

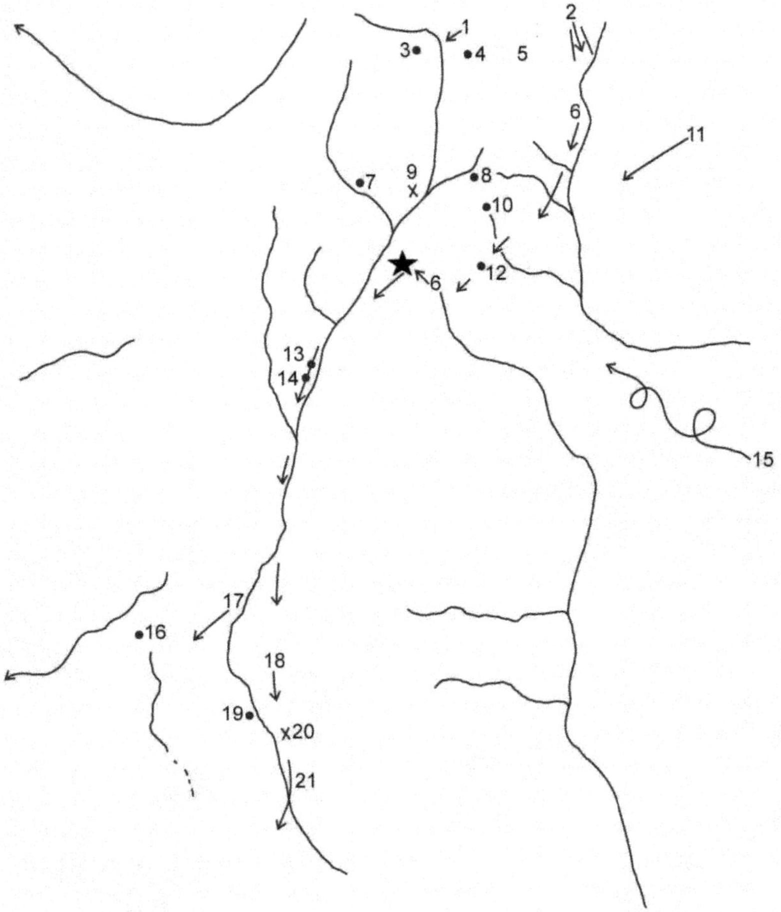

1. Pike's Stockade
2. Raton Pass
3. Antonito
4. San Luis
5. Maxwell Land Grant
6. Santa Fe Trail
7. Abiquiu
8. Taos
9. Embudo Battle
10. Mora
11. Cimarron Cutoff
12. Las Vegas
13. Los Lunas
14. Belen
15. Texas-New Mexico Expedition
16. Santa Rita
17. Kearney's Route
18. Chihuahua Trail
19. Mesilla
20. Battle of Brazito
21. Doniphan's Route
   To Mexico

★ Santa Fe

1806 to 1850- The Mexican Period

4

War Most Uncivil

The U.S. armed the local militias in order to better control the nomads. It also deployed its regular army and built several forts in nomad territory. The U.S. government began scientifically surveying the land and established American-style government, appointing territorial governors. By all rights New Mexico should have become a state by 1860, but issues of slavery, race, religion and use of resources intervened.

The Catholic Church saw that New Mexico had been somewhat ignored and now needed its own bishop, so French-born Jean Baptiste Lamy was sent from Ohio to Santa Fe in 1850. He would become one of the State's most famous citizens. He set about the business of civilizing what he saw as a backward region. Civilization meant schools, gardens, hospitals, new churches, more clergy, and paved streets and railroads, among other things.

He also sought to strengthen the Church. The Protestants were recruiting among the natives.

In 1861 civil war broke out over slavery. An army of Texans invaded New Mexico, and by March 1862 had taken Albuquerque and Santa Fe. As they marched toward Fort Union north of Las Vegas they were met and defeated by a Union army at Glorieta Pass. They were driven back down the Rio Grande to Texas, which safeguarded the gold fields of the West.

The Union army turned its attention to the Apaches and Navajos. In 1863-65 the Mescalero Apaches and the Navajos were forced to end their nomadic life with a brief, unsuccessful attempt to settle them on a reservation on the Pecos River called *Bosque Redondo*. Both were returned to their home areas by 1868, the Navajos completing their "Long Walk" back to the Four Corners. They each signed treaties agreeing to peace thereafter, which they lived up to. In 1863 Abraham Lincoln recognized the citizenship of the Pueblos by issuing them *canes of office* for their governors.

Navajo shepherdess tends her flock in solitude on the reservation. Illustration from *The Story of the American Indian* by Eldridge S. Brooks, 1887.

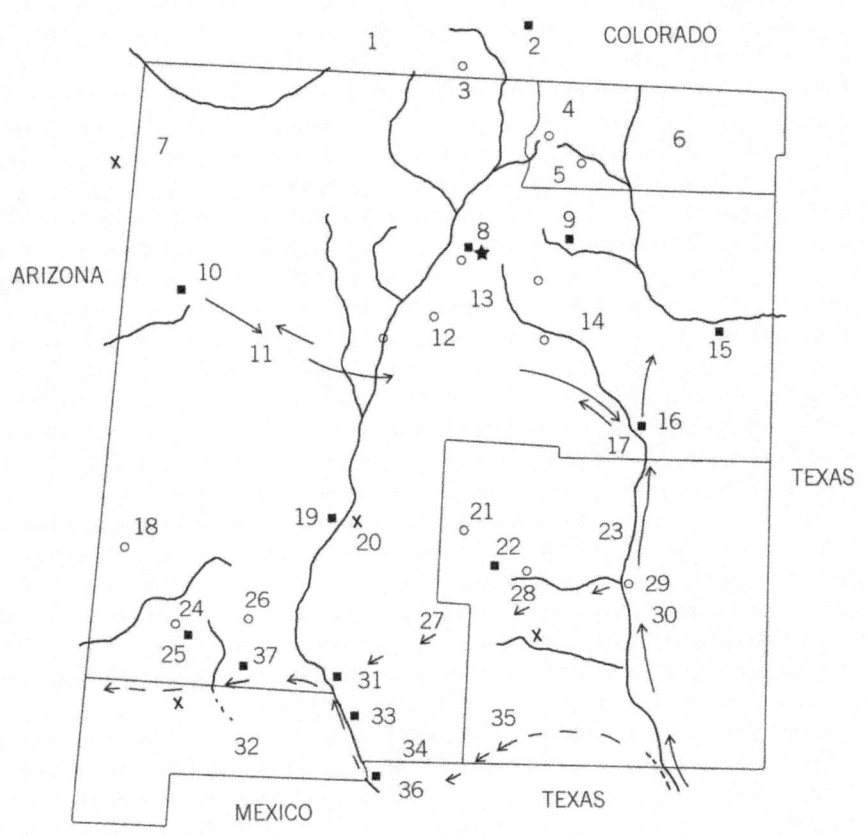

1. New Mexico Irredenta
2. Ft. Garlnd
3. 37N
4. Elizabeth Town
5. Cimarron
6. Colfax Country
7. Canyon de Chelly
8. Ft. Marcy
9. Ft. Union
10. Ft. Wingate
11. Long Walk
12. Golden
13. Glorieta
14. Anton Chico
15. Ft. Bascom
16. Ft. Sumner
17. Bosque Redondo
18. Mogollon
19. Ft. Craig
20. Valverde
21. White Oaks
22. Ft. Stanton
23. Lincoln County
24. Silver City
25. Ft. Bayard
26. Kingston-Hillsboro
27. Chisum Trail
28. Lincoln
29. Chisum Ranch
30. Goodnight-Loving Trail
31. Ft. Selden
32. Galsden Purchase
33. Ft. Fillmore
34. 32N
35. Butterfield Stage Line
36. Ft. Bliss
37. Ft. Cummings
★ Santa Fe

WILD WEST NEW MEXICO 1850 - 1890

Wars x   Forts ■   Trails →

5

The Wild West

Now things got complicated! The United States, reunited, with slavery ended, entered the era of full-scale industrialization based on a capitalist economic system and an abundance of resources. Many of those resources lay in the West. People sought wealth through their acquisition and use. The U.S. was about to become a world power.

The common symbolic representation of the Anglo in the tri-cultural mythos has been a prospector armed with a pick. Between 1865 and 1915 every corner of New Mexico was examined for gold. In the mountains gold, silver, copper and coal were found. Towns sprang up, and fell down again, dotting the landscape with ghost towns.

Investors, often foreigners, brought money to build railroads, mines, ranches and other businesses. Coal at Raton, Madrid and

Gallup fueled the new transcontinental railroads which stretched into New Mexico in the 1880s. One could travel to St. Louis in days instead of months. All manner of new building materials were brought in. The forests here provided lumber, ties, telegraph poles, and fence posts, which could be transported out to the world as well. So could agricultural products, mainly sheep and cattle.

Water, what there was of it, became more important. Steam engines and mines needed it. Cattle and crops needed it. A growing population needed it. It was worth fighting over, whether in court, the legislature or with six guns.

The ethos of the new nation was that of laissez faire free enterprise individualistic capitalism intended to let people prosper through hard work, intelligence, inventiveness, and Darwinian fitness which, sometimes, was manifested in crooked behavior. The U.S. homestead laws applied to the vast lands opened up and there was no place for communal ownership. Land was a commodity and a resource. The old land grants came under attack. Some survived, some did not.

This ethos spawned entrepreneurs — businessmen raising themselves by their own bootstraps by means fair and foul. The fear of failure was great, and the rules were still being written. The Santa Fe Ring was the local manifestation of the National Game. The game pitted the rich against the poor and the poor against the poor. Immigrants flooded America, becoming the labor force and, sometimes, rich men themselves. They dug the mines, built the railroads, settled the homesteads, started businesses, and many of them failed. We remember the successes mainly.

Who understands today that New Mexico's citizens were merely a part of this great game? By the 1870s Colfax and Lincoln

Counties were major examples of this American Dynamism gone somewhat berserk. Each county had land, lots of land, some water, some gold, and diverse peoples wanting to make a living from those resources. War broke out in both counties.

Irishmen, a Scot, a German, Texas cowboys, Spanish farmers, Apaches, some Black soldiers and an Englishman, John Henry Tunstall, struggled to control the huge southeast corner of New Mexico known as Lincoln County. When Tunstall was killed in 1879 it set off events about which much of the world knows today. It produced New Mexico's single most famous person.

A cowboy working for Tunstall, young William Bonney Antrim, got revenge on the Irish sheriff and others. He was eventually hunted down and shot by a Texas-born sheriff, Pat Garrett, whose daughter, Elizabeth Garrett, would later write the state song of New Mexico. More has been written and filmed about Billy The Kid than most other New Mexicans put together. A host of psychiatrists might be able to explain why.

Others died over water, rangeland and livestock. When Judge Albert Fountain of Mesilla disappeared near the White Sands, rancher Oliver Lee was accused of murdering him. Lee was at war with his neighbors over water and cattle and they wanted the courts to stop him. The courts acquitted him and Fountain remains missing. Lee lived to be an old man and state senator in the 1930s.

The railroads doomed the wild buffalo and the cavalry drove the Comanche and Jicarilla Apaches to reservations. The large mines at Santa Rita, in the middle of Apacheria, created more conflict. The army, with Apache help, drove Geronimo and others onto reservations. More than half of the men in the army were immigrants, mostly Irish and German, and African Americans known as Buffalo Soldiers made up another large component. Other African Americans came as cowboys and farmers. One of those cowboys found the first evidence of the Folsom people.

In policies consistent with national attitudes in general, Indian children were sent to school. Few kids liked school, and schools were run on a Prussian model where readin, writin and rithmetic were taught to the tune of a hickory stick. The nation was engaged in one of the great experiments of all history. It was trying to create one nation, indivisible, out of all the peoples on earth, and there was no model for this effort. At Dawson, for instance, how else were Slavs, Irishmen, Germans, Arabs, Italians, Mexicans, Welshmen and a few Chinese, among others, to become united Americans if not through education?

By the 1890s New Mexico was chartering colleges and universities and creating public schools and other institutions. The various churches had already opened many schools. Bilingualism was a moot point. Citizenship first required a common language. Many of the colleges were intended to prepare teachers. Others would develop engineers, nurses, mechanics and farmer/ranchers to function in the new world of science.

By the 1890s the idea had taken root in America that its huge arid west could be developed if water could be found for irrigation. Iron windmills were fine for livestock and gardens, but reservoirs, canals and dams were needed for the real work. New Mexico was a prime location to prove this idea.

A major project began on the Pecos River. Streams all over the territory were tapped to water land which would be sold to small farmers and to businesses. Plans to dam the Rio Grande were drawn up. The resulting Elephant Butte Dam and Lake weren't completed until 1915. It provided electricity, flood control and a large-scale chile industry in the Hatch Valley. Farmers, often immigrants, were drawn into the open lands to raise dry land beans, broom corn and livestock. Eastern New Mexico especially filled with people hoping to fulfill the American dream. They believed the theory that rain would follow the plow, and because New Mexico has wet and dry cycles, their dream seemed possible.

An interesting interlude. In 1898 the U.S. and Spain went to war over Cuba and the Philippines. A wild New Yorker who loved the West came to New Mexico to recruit a regiment of cavalry. He needed men who could already ride and shoot. His 1st U.S. Volunteer Cavalry fought at San Juan Hill, became famous as the Rough Riders, and he became President of the U.S. Five of New Mexico's 33 counties bear names connected with those events. Theodore Roosevelt was a friend of New Mexico thereafter and supported statehood, which still took another twelve years to accomplish due to party politics and the sense that New Mexico was different. A majority of its people were Spanish and Indian—and Catholic—in a time when the United States sank to its lowest point in terms of bigotry. Finally a constitution was agreed upon in 1910, and in January 1912 New Mexico became the 47th state in the Union. The first state flag, designed by Ralph Emerson Twitchell, was a bright blue field trimmed in gold fringe with a small U.S. flag in the upper left corner and the New Mexico State Seal in the lower right hand corner. "NEW MEXICO" was embroidered diagonally across the blue field from the lower left hand corner to the upper right hand corner. It speaks volumes about the world's image of New Mexico. It was an exotic place still in need of civilizing.

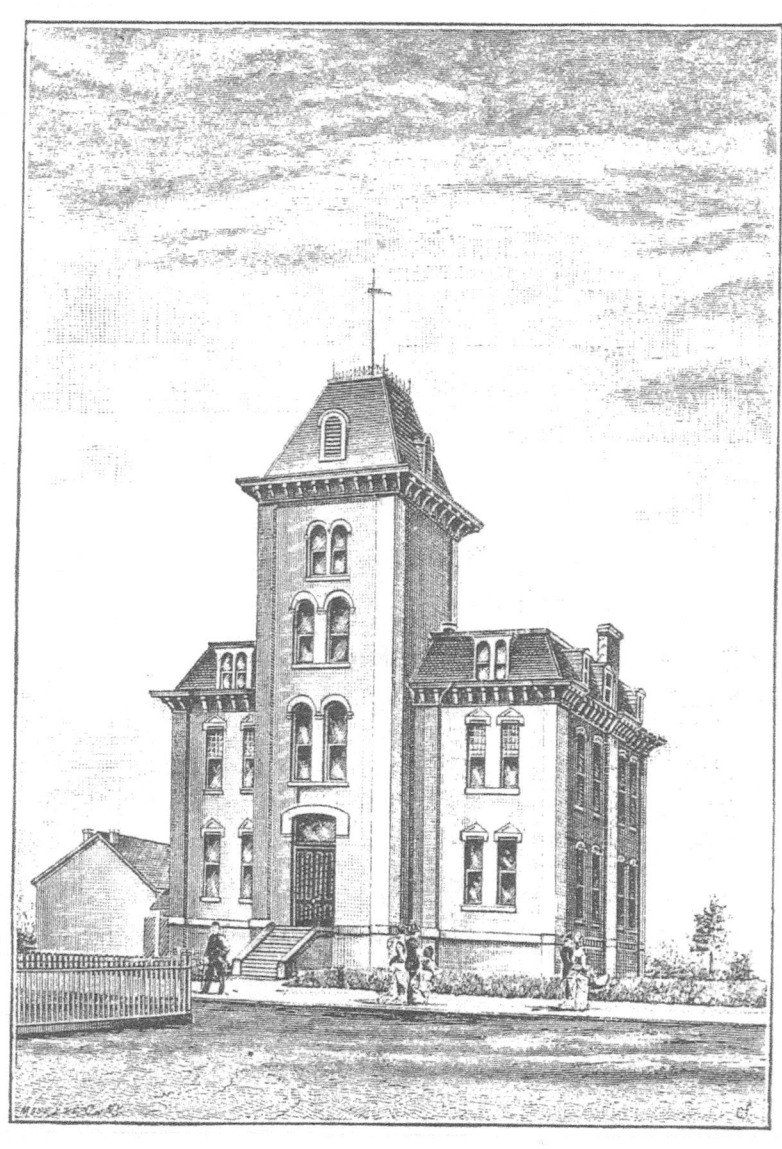

This high school was Santa Fe's Pride in the 1890s. Illustration from *New Mexico* **by Max Frost, 1894.**

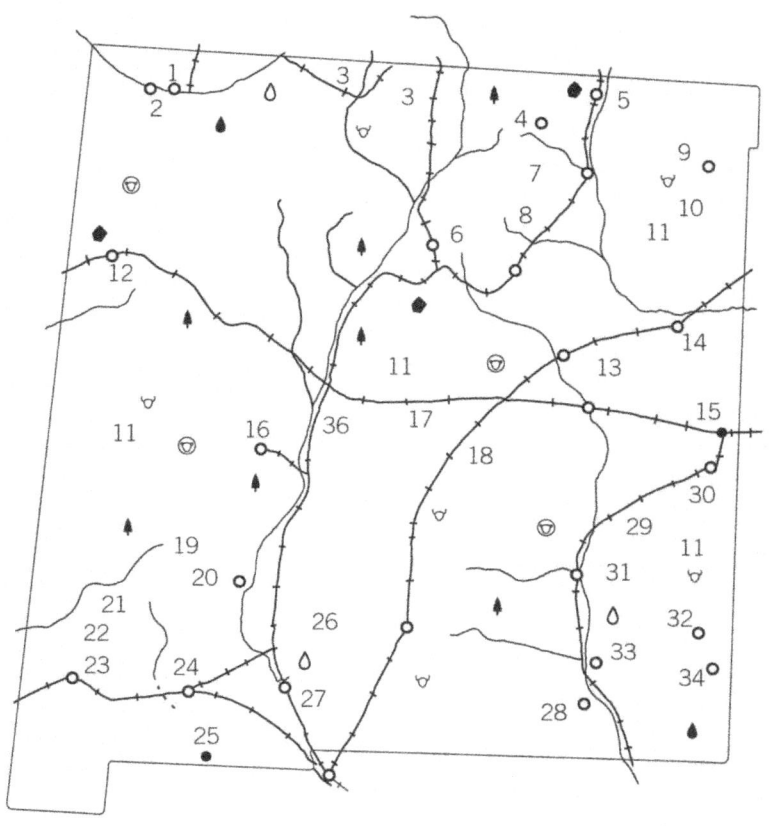

1. Bloomfield
2. Farmington
3. DRGW
4. Dawson
5. Raton
6. Pecos NW
7. Springer
8. AT & SF
9. Clayton
10. Kiowa NG
11. Dry Land Farming
12. Gallup
13. Santa Rosa
14. Tucumcari
15. Clovis
16. Magdalena
17. AT & SF
18. SPRI
19. Aldo Leopold NW
20. Hot Springs
21. Silver
22. Copper
23. Lordsburg
24. Deming
25. Columbus
26. Alamogordo
27. Las Cruces
28. Carlsbad
29. AT & SF
30. Portales
31. Roswell
32. Lovington
33. Artesia
34. Hobbs

NEW MEXICO 1890-1920

Railroads Ca. 1900

Irrigation ⬨   Cattle ⩗   Sheep ⊖

Oil ⬩   Coal ⬢   Forests ⬧

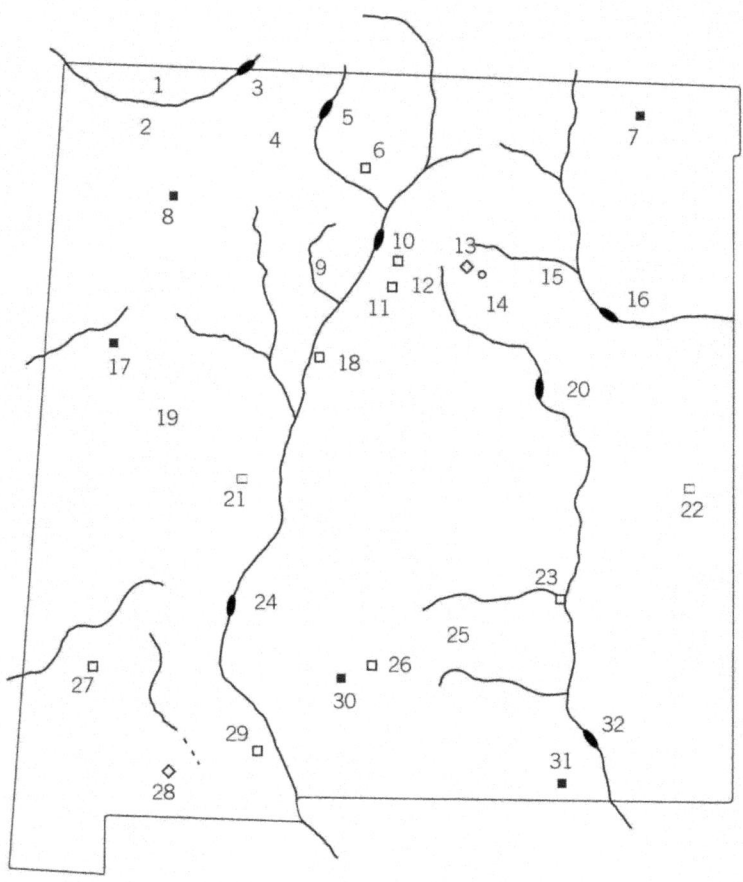

1. Ute Reservation
2. Navajo Reservation
3. Navajo Lake
4. Jicarilla Apache Reservation
5. El Vado Lake
6. El Rito Normal (Northern)
7. Mt. Capulin NM
8. Chaco Canyon National Monument
9. Cochiti Lake
10. NM Deaf
11. State Pen
12. College of Santa Fe
13. Camp Luna
14. NM Highlands
15. NM Mental Hospital
16. Conchas Lake
17. El Morro NM
18. UNM
19. Navajo Reservations
20. Ft. Summer Lake
21. NM Tech (Mines)
22. Eastern NM
23. NM Military
24. Elephant Butte Lake
25. Mescale Reservation
26. NM Blind
27. Western NM
28. Camp Cody
29. NMSU (A&M)
30. White Sands NM
31. Carlsbad Caverns NP
32. Lake McMillan

Dams and Lakes ●   Military Posts ◇

Schools ☐   Parks and Monuments ■

40

6

Unforeseen Change

However the exoticism turned out to be a plus. By the 1890s the railroads were bringing people to New Mexico, usually on their way to California. This included creative types otherwise known as artists. They fell for the place. Tourists bought curios, which the railroads encouraged natives to make. The business of jewelry, textiles and pottery had begun.

The artists tended to stay. This exotic place had beautiful light, clear blue skies, lots of sun, seasons and scenery galore. There were enchanting Indians, cowboys and Spanish folks to paint, write about, wax poetic over, and study. Santa Fe and Taos became art colonies and the center of anthropological studies. Ancient ruins were everywhere, waiting for the new scientists called archaeologists to dig them up.

New Mexico already had a historical society. Now it gained a history museum in the Palace of the Governors and a fine arts museum in 1917. Frijoles Canyon, Chaco Canyon and the Gila Cliff Dwellings came to the attention of men like Adolph Bandelier, a German-Swiss archaeologist.

Another movement was afoot. Theodore Roosevelt created a national forest system in 1906. The Lincoln National Forest was one of the first in the country and others followed. Not everyone was happy with this, as it limited use of the forest areas by ranchers, lumbermen and others. The national parks and monuments system was also expanded. The Carlsbad Caverns were discovered and quickly made part of that system. By the 1920s the nation's first wilderness area was designated in the Gila River headwaters.

The high, dry air of New Mexico brought people seeking cures for lung diseases. They were called health seekers. Tuberculosis sanatoriums sprang up all over the state. Two famous artists became New Mexicans in this way. Will Shuster would create Zozobra, symbol of the Santa Fe Fiesta. (In the short time since this was first written it has been discovered that Shuster got the idea in part while talking to two women friends, so now he has to share the credit. That's the way history goes, folks.) John Gaw Meem would become a force in the creation of neo-pueblo/territorial architectural styles. These artists saw that adobe-style building made with modern building materials fit the landscape far better than the brick and frame structures Americans had preached for years as symbols of modernization.

The Indian schools taught painting, starting a new generation of artists. Anthropologists encouraged the revival of fine pottery making. In the 1930s the WPA art programs kept alive the work of painters and writers while encouraging the pursuit of the Spanish Colonial art styles. Men and women of national reputation settled in New Mexico. These included Peter Hurd and Paul Horgan in the Roswell area and Georgia O'Keeffe at Abiquiu.

In 1910 Mexico suffered another revolution. Thousands of Mexicans fled north, working on railroads and in mines and on farms, especially in southern New Mexico. The U.S. became involved in what was a civil war compounded by foreign influences. In 1916 one of the revolutionaries, Pancho Villa, attacked Columbus, New Mexico. By this time World War I was two years old. Americans were becoming paranoid about foreign attack and some saw Mexico as a path for German and Japanese invasion of the U.S.

The U.S. sent an expedition into Mexico to catch Villa while the New Mexico National Guard protected the border. The expedition failed, but made General John Pershing famous enough to be placed in command of the American army when the U.S. entered World War I in 1917, which it did in part over fears concerning German overtures to Mexico.

Several thousand New Mexicans went into the military where as many died from flu and accidents as did from shells and bullets in France. At home the paranoid hysteria created by the war was evident. Particularly suspect were the Mexicans, the Austro-Hungarian miners, and anyone who spoke positively about Germany. Draft dodgers were treated harshly. That hysteria accounted for some dark episodes. The general economy also contributed to the hysteria and those fears continued beyond war's end.

Nature increased fears, for once again the erratic but generally dry climate struck. In the late teens and 1920s drought descended on New Mexico. Farmers lost the farm, all over the state. The livestock industry suffered. Herds had to be moved out of state. It became apparent that sheep—those of the Navajo included—were denuding the land.

Coal miners struck at Raton and Gallup, with occasional violence resulting. The National Guard was sent in to keep peace. Fear of communism became the new hysteria. Oil was discovered in southeastern and northwestern New Mexico, promising a new source of jobs and income. Hobbs was born. New Mexico became part of one of the great political scandals of that era when Albert Fall of Mesilla became Secretary of the Interior, gave his friends access to the Teapot Dome Naval oil reserve, and went to prison for it.

Another piece of related darkness followed. As the nation demanded an end to free immigration and in some places prohibition of the sale of alcohol, New Mexico reversed its liberal policy regarding school integration in 1925. Local districts could segregate dark-skinned students. The KKK appeared in Little Texas, and the Catholic Church came under attack because it seemed to support the use of alcohol and religious orders were allowed to teach in some public schools. Chicago gangsters bought hideout ranches in the mountains of New Mexico where locals were making moonshine.

When the Great Depression began, New Mexico was already generally depressed, but the Dust Bowl drought further hammered the economy. Northeastern New Mexico suffered especially and many people left, mainly for California. The land was littered with ghost towns again. The Navajo had to be convinced to reduce their herds, as did other ranchers. Banks failed. Other banks foreclosed on farms and businesses. New Mexico went for The New Deal.

The WPA and CCC provided jobs and income. The REA provided electricity to those who had not had it. Electricity meant contact with the outside world, water pumps, reading at night and appliances. Paved highways, new buildings, schools, conservation efforts, dams, more water and art all flowed from these programs.

Highway 66 was realigned and paved in the 1930s. It carried Okies fleeing the Dust Bowl as well as tourists. The oil towns boomed and their gasoline fed the growing number of autos and trucks and tractors. Heating oil and natural gas began to replace coal, so the mines waned.

Science came slowly to New Mexico. Robert Oppenheimer bought a ranch in the Pecos Wilderness for health reasons in 1927. Charles Lindbergh visited Santa Fe that year. He was soon mapping Chaco Canyon from the air. Robert Goddard chose Roswell to test his rockets. The University of New Mexico Lobos were the first football team in the nation to fly to a game. Senator Bronson Cutting was killed in a plane crash. Aldous Huxley sited part of his novel *Brave New World* in New Mexico. Change was in the air.

Between 1900 and 1940 the most popular symbol used in New Mexico was the Indian swastika, which symbolized good fortune. Even after the Zia sun symbol was chosen for the new state flag, the swastika was far more widely used. That was about to change, also.

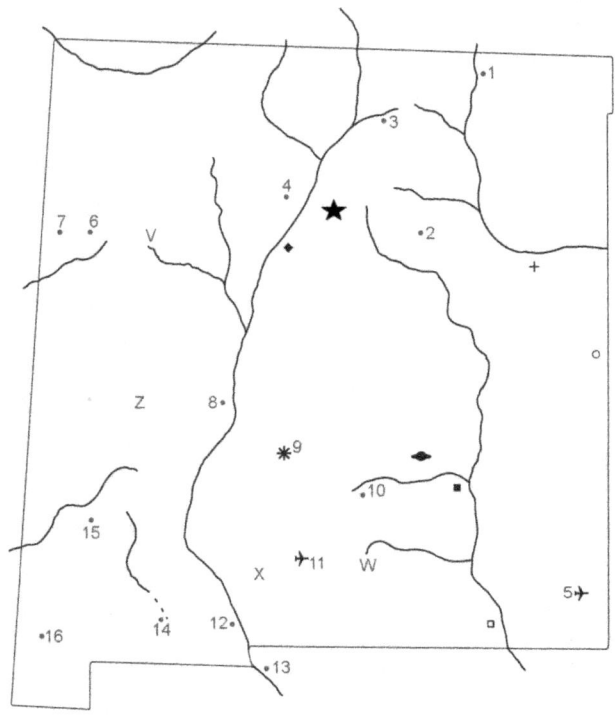

★ Santa Fe
  Bruns Army Hospital
  Japanese Internment Camp
  200th C
  804th TD HQ

◆ Albuquerque
  Kirtland Air Force Base
  200th A,B,Band, Medical
  Sandia National Laboratory
  120th Eng. A

■ Roswell
  Roswell-Walker Air Force Base
  804th A
  Orchard Park POW Camp

○ Clovis
  Clovis-Cannon Air Force Base
  200th E

\+ Tucumcari
  804th TD C
  and Medical

◻ Carlsbad
  Carlsbad Air Force Base
  200th E

1. 804th B
2. 120th Eng. C
3. 200th H
4. Los Alamos
5. Hobbs Air Force Base
6. Ft. Wingate Ordinance Depot
7. 200th D
8. 120th Eng. B
9. Trinity Site

10. Ft. Stanton POW
11. Alamogordo-Holloman AFB
12. 120th Eng. HQ
13. Ft. Bliss
14. 200th HQ
15. 200th G
16. Lordsburg POW

V. Uranium Mines
W. Sunspot Observatory UFO Site
X. White Sands
Z. VLA Radio Telescopes

WORLD WAR II AND COLD WAR NEW MEXICO
The New Mexico National Guard consisted of the: 200th Coast Artillery (AA), 804th Tank Destroyer Battalion and 120th Engineer Battalion

7

On the World Stage

In 1940 the U.S. had 132,127,000 people. New Mexico had 531,818, or one of every 242 Americans. New York City alone had sixteen times as many citizens in an area which could be lost easily in a corner of most New Mexico counties. New Mexico still had a foot in the distant past. It had the worst infant mortality rate in the nation and one of the very lowest education rates, but the world was changing, and New Mexico is part of the world.

In 1939 the New Mexico National Guard gave up their horses and became anti-aircraft gunners, engineers and manned anti-tank units. As Hitler perverted the swastika and Japan threatened all of Asia, the government called up the 200th Coast Artillery Regiment for duty in the Philippines. Many of its men had joined the Guard during the Depression for its pay and its camaraderie. Every community knew a guardsman. Four months after Pearl

Harbor those men still living surrendered and endured the hell of the Bataan Death March and of prison camps to become New Mexico's best known military group. Of roughly 1800, about 900 survived. The rest of the Guard went to Europe, fighting in Italy, France and Germany. Thousands more New Mexicans served all over the world in all the services, receiving an education in the process. Navajo Code Talkers and Spanish lawyers at Nuremberg, Anglo airmen and sailors of all stripes, most of whom had never seen the sea, exemplify how New Mexico did more than its fair share.

In 1941 President Franklin Delano Roosevelt created the Manhattan Project to pursue the development of a nuclear weapon. Robert Oppenheimer was the physicist chosen to head the project, and he had to pick a secretive place for a laboratory. Remembering the Los Alamos Ranch School he had visited in the 1920s, he chose it. The army and scientists moved in during 1942. Three years later they tested a bomb on the Alamogordo bombing range—not in Alamogordo—but rather in the Jornada del Muerto. This weapon definitely ended World War II. It changed the world, too. Spies had already taken its secrets to the USSR, the United States' next rival.

The economy of New Mexico was altered by government spending on a large scale. The New Mexico skies were perfect for flight training. Air bases were built and many thousands of American fliers learned their skills over those vast empty spaces. Three of those bases remain into the Twenty-First Century. Hospitals, POW camps, munition dumps and oil fields employed more people. Many of the newcomers would remain after peace returned.

The state was also home to a Japanese internment camp in

Santa Fe. The hysteria born of war once again led the U.S. to less than honorable behavior. While the state touted racial harmony, racism was very much alive, and the events of the Bataan Death March made it worse. The battleship *New Mexico* was hit by a kamikaze. She and the cruiser *Santa Fe* served with distinction across the Pacific.

Two of the most beloved journalists of the war period called New Mexico home. Young cartoonist Bill Mauldin of Mountain Park won a Pulitzer Prize for his work across Europe. Correspondent Ernie Pyle, an adopted son, wrote the stories of the common soldiers. He was killed late in the war on a Pacific island.

A vintage postcard showing Ernie Pyle and his home in Albuquerque. The home is now a library.

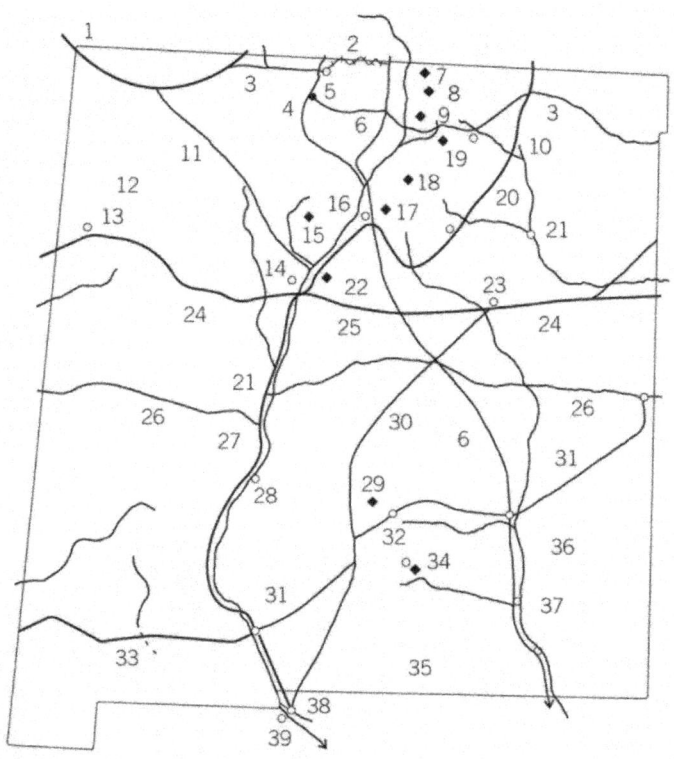

1. Four Corners
2. Cumbres and Toltec RR
3. US 64
4. Tierra Amarilla
5. Chama
6. US 285
7. Ski Rio
8. Red River
9. Taos
10. Philmont Boy Scout Ranch
11. US 550
12. Hillerman Country
13. Indian Ceremonial
14. Int. Balloon Festival
15. Pajarito
16. Opera
17. Santa Fe
18. Sipapu
19. Angel Fire
20. I-25
21. Sabinoso Wilderness
22. Sandia
23. Blue Hole Scuba Site
24. I-40
25. Hwy 66
26. US 60
27. US 85
28. Bosque del Apache NWR
29. Ski Apache
30. US 54
31. US 70
32. Ruidoso
33. I-10
34. Cloudcroft
35. Otero Mesa
36. Little Texas
37. Football Kingdom
38. El Paso
39. Juarez

NEW MEXICO 1945-2005

Ski Areas ◆

8

The New World

In August 1945 it ended, the men came home, and New Mexico stepped into the future. The U.S. government brought a group of Hitler's rocket scientists to Alamogordo, thereby creating White Sands Missile Range and the American space program. Soon thereafter, in 1947, a spacecraft manned by aliens reportedly crashed sort of near Roswell.

In that year a Pueblo Indian veteran sued to regain his right to vote and got it. Veterans of the 10th Mountain Division looked at possibilities for ski areas in New Mexico's mountains and found them. Lots of veterans went to college on the G.I. Bill. There was no going back.

In 1951–1952 school leaders, many of them veterans, joined with African American leaders to desegregate those New Mexico schools separated 25 years earlier. As the complexion of things changed, a fourth culture began gaining a voice and a stage. This was immediately noticeable in sports.

A national weapons laboratory was established in Albuquerque, a solar observatory near Cloudcroft, and interstate highways inched forward. They would bring still more tourists. A world-class opera opened in Santa Fe and the New Mexico art market became one of the largest in the world. The motion picture industry found New Mexico to be photogenic. Smokey The Bear was born in the Capitan Mountains.

The story of Smokey is indicative of an ongoing fact of geography: periods of serious drought lead to serious forest fires. The agricultural community struggled as it depleted much of the groundwater available and had to share water with neighboring states. The population using water quadrupled between 1940 and 2000.

Hippies appeared in the 1960s–1970s, drawn by the environment and a perceived simpler life style. Some stayed to become the seed of an environmental movement. They also introduced new religious/spiritual ideas to an already interesting matrix. New immigrants would further add to that mix.

In turn, old groups had to search for their identity in an even more rapidly changing world. Those of Spanish origin found voices through representative authors as did some Indians. Names changed, just to keep things confusing—once *Spanish*, then *Mexican*, then *Spanish-Americans*, then *Chicanos*—the people of Spanish origin became *Hispanics*. Even Anglos began looking more closely at their origins. Turns out a lot of them were Italian, German, Polish, Greek, Jewish, Irish, Lebanese or Scots. In fact a few were Japanese or Chinese.

On a darker note, violence could erupt, as it did in 1967 at Tierra Amarilla over land issues, or at the state penitentiary in 1980 over socio/political issues. Social problems of poverty, poor education, drug misuse, and drunk driving cast New Mexico into the low end of many ratings and the state continues to pursue answers. During the Vietnam War, New Mexico had the third highest ratio of war deaths in the nation. No ethnic or racial group was singled out, but the poor, as is usual in frontier wars, were hit harder.

We Grow as We Go says the state motto. We have cast rockets, balloons, and radio waves into the heavens. More importantly, in New Mexico Indians dance for water, Spanish-American Catholics pray to appropriate saints for water, and Anglos drill, dig, and dam and pray for water. We all lift our eyes to the heavens for sight of clouds, rain, snow and rainbows, for as Mary Austin and Ross Calvin separately noted, this is the *land of little rain. . .where sky determines*.

The Oñate Conquest of 1598–1600. Illustration by José Cisneros from *Chavez, A Distinctive American Clan of New Mexico* by Fray Angélico Chávez. Sunstone Press, 2009.

Timeline

10000 years ago	Folsom type people
1000 years ago	Chaco people
1400s AD	Athapascan peoples
1540	Coronado
1598	Oñate's colony
1680	Pueblo Revolt
1693	DeVargas' reconquest
1706	Albuquerque founded
1776	DeAnza in office
1806	Zebulon Pike's visit
1821	Mexican Independence and Santa Fe Trail
1837	Revolt against Governor Perez
1841	Texas-New Mexico Expedition
1846	Kearney captured New Mexico
1847	Taos Rebellion
1850	New Mexico a U.S. Territory, Archbishop Lamy arrived in Santa Fe

1853	Gadsden Purchase
1862	Battle of Glorieta
1864	Navajos to Bosque Redondo
1868	Navajo peace treaty, end of Long Walk
1879	Lincoln County War began
1881	S.F. Railroad reached Santa Fe, Billy the Kid killed
1886	Geronimo captured
1889	UNM and NMSU chartered
1898	Rough Riders to Cuba
1906	National forests created
1912	New Mexico finally a state
1916	Pancho Villa's raid
1917	Fine arts museum
1927	Lindbergh and Oppenheimer in New Mexico
1933	New Deal art programs
1937	Highway 66 paved
1941	200th Coast Artillery to Philippines
1942	Bataan Death March
1945	Trinity Test
1947	Roswell Incident
1952	School desegregation
1967	Tierra Amarilla courthouse raid
1980	Penitentiary riot
2012	Centennial of statehood

Guide For Teachers

1. Do not get tangled up in standards. Learn New Mexico history and teach it well.

2. No single test or assignment should count for many points; therefore, a bad day should not destroy any student's grade. Quizzes and assignments should be considered as rehearsal or practice for the final. Students should know what they are going to be tested over from day one.

3. Vocabulary is one of the most important things you can teach because it is the essence of all knowledge. We know our world by its names. The list included is not all inclusive. It is intended to support research and all materials you use. Feel free to add to it.

4. You need to have New Mexico atlases in your classroom. Demand them. Also have a copy of *New Mexico Place Names*

handy. Devote one day a week, preferably Friday, to geography. Throw in statistical information when you can.

5. Students should be expected to conduct research to fill in details. Every sub-unit should involve research assignments using books, the ever-increasing internet sources available, and local resources such as museums, elders, and historical societies. A social science fair is a good thing.

6. These essential questions should be the focus of study:

   * How has geography—climate and resources—affected New Mexico history? Remember that geography is the stage and history is the play.

   * Who are the New Mexicans? (How has cultural diversity happened and affected New Mexico history?)

   * What role has science and technology played in New Mexico history?

   * How have events on the world stage affected New Mexico history?

   * What role have the arts played in New Mexico history?

Glossary

These words are important for understanding New Mexico history, whether they are used in this text or not.

abajo:	Below
aboriginal:	First inhabitants of an area
acequia:	An irrigation ditch and its owners
agenda:	An underlying idea or belief
Aggies:	Agricultural students and New Mexico State University types
alamo:	Cottonwood tree
alcalde:	Local leader, mayor perhaps
Anasazi:	Navajo for *Our Ancient Enemy* – applied to ancient Pueblo peoples
Anglo:	English, English speaking
annex:	To add to by taking over
anthropology:	The study of human development
archaeology:	The study of artifacts/physical evidence from the past
armada:	Military fleet
arriba:	Above, upper

artesian:	Ground water which surfaces naturally, with force
artifact:	Any item from the past which serves as evidence
Athabascan:	Language group including Navajos and Apaches
Bataan:	Where the New Mexico National Guard were captured in the Philippines
bias:	Showing favor or disfavor for something
bohemian:	Artistic, unconventional
Buffalo Soldiers:	African American soldiers of the 1865-1918 period
butte:	A small, steep-sided hill surrounded by flattish terrain
caballero:	Horseman, knight, gentleman
camino:	Road
carpetbagger:	Post Civil War term for those who migrated and took advantage of those among whom they settled
casta:	Social class or caste
Chicano:	A word in search of a meaning—sort of means Mexican/Mestizo
civilized:	Having a high degree of arts, science, technology, a written language and supposedly civil behavior
clan:	A subdivision of a tribe
condescending:	Coming down to a lower level
confabulation:	Making up stories or details which are not true
culture:	A body of customs, beliefs, and behaviors practiced by a given people
desert:	A very dry area, not necessarily hot
Dine':	Navajo name for themselves—*The People*
discrimination:	Making choices (only bad if done unfairly)
don:	Sir, lord
doña:	Lady
dragoons:	Heavy cavalry
drought:	A long, excessively dry period
dynamic:	Energetic, forceful, creating change
entrepreneur:	One who creates business enterprises in search of profit

ethnic:	Divisions of mankind based on language, religion and customs
ethos:	A set of strongly held beliefs
escarpment:	A steep-sloped edge of a plateau
fandango:	A public dance
gringo:	Name given to people from the U.S. at the time of the Mexican War
hidalgo:	A minor nobleman
Hispanic:	Of Spanish origin—has become an umbrella term
historiography:	The study of how history is written or told
hysteria:	Unreasonable fear
Iberia:	The Spanish peninsula
indigenous:	Native of an area; it is similar to aboriginal—use carefully
inquisition:	A severe questioning—implies torture
kachina:	An Indian god, or impersonation of or carving of a god
Keresan:	A pueblo language group
kiva:	A pueblo religious building (there are no kiva fireplaces in modern homes
Koshare:	Pueblo religious clowns/teachers/policemen
llano:	Plains
la bajada:	Going down place—escarpment
las animas:	The souls
legend:	Pretty much the same as myth
Lobos:	Wolves and University of New Mexico types
mesa:	A small, flat-topped mountain
mestizo:	One of mixed European and Indian ancestry
militia:	Citizen soldiers serving for local defense
Moor:	Term applied to the Moslem invader of Spain in the middle ages
myth:	A story with a kernel of truth at its center
nomadic:	Moving about, most of the time in search of food

Okies:	Great Plains farmers who were refugees from the Dust Bowl and the Great Depression
Paranoid:	Fearful of being attacked
patrón:	Aristocratic leader
penitente:	One who practices penance as a religious rite
peón:	Lower class servant of the aristocracy
plateau:	A large, relatively level highland
plaza:	Town square, *The Place*
political ring:	Politicians who seek to exploit the resources and people of a given place
Pre-Columbian:	Before Columbus came to America
presidio:	Fort
primitive:	At the first stages of development
prospector:	One who searches for wealth—gold, for instance
pueblo:	Spanish for *village* or *people;* broad name for sedentary villages of Indians
race:	Major divisions of mankind based on physical features
rain shadow:	Deserts created when mountains block out moisture from the sea
real:	Royal
resources:	Those things mankind uses for survival
río:	River
romanticize:	To believe that some people, or an earlier time, are superior to us
sanatorium:	A residential medical facility for treating certain illnesses
santa, santo:	Holy
santa, san:	Saint
savage:	The opposite of civilized
sedentary:	Staying in one place for a long time
Sephardim:	Jewish inhabitants of Iberia
sierra:	Mountain range

sipapu:	Mythical place where pueblo peoples emerged from the underworld
specious:	A false claim
swastika:	An ancient, universal, good luck symbol, much used by Native Americans and early peoples all over the world
Tanoan:	Pueblo language group, subdivided into Tewa, Tiwa and Towa
totem:	A symbol considered to have magical properties (team mascots)
tribe:	A relatively small group who claim a common ancestor
vaquero:	Cowboy
viceroy:	King's representative
Zunian:	A pueblo language group (so is Hopi, but they are Arizonans)
Zia:	A Keresan pueblo from whence comes the state sun symbol on the flag
zozobra:	Gloom, despair

Words must be understood contextually and in terms of common sense. The dictionary does not always provide us these factors. There are words like *savage* or *swastika* which carry heavy emotional baggage. They must be addressed in an intelligent fashion.

Author's Suggested New Mexico Reading List

The best way to increase one's knowledge of New Mexico history is through reading. Teachers should lobby their school districts and colleges to give academic credit for serious reading pursuits. Likewise, students should be required to be acquainted with books.

At the risk of offending many people, I offer the following list. Remember that the issue of which works are best is a matter of opinion; this is my list, which is by no means all inclusive. These works will give a reader a foundation for building on as a lifelong student of this most interesting part of the world. The list is actually endless. Also see the list of fifty-plus books on New Mexico from Sunstone Press that follows my list.

Fiction:

Anaya, Rudolfo. *Bless Me Ultima.*
Arnold, Elliot. *Time of the Gringo.*
Bandelier, Adolph. *The Delight Makers.* *
Blacker, Irwin. *Taos.*
Bradford, Richard. *Red Sky at Morning.*
Hillerman, Tony. *Dance Hall of the Dead.*
La Farge, Oliver. *The Enemy Gods.* *
Laughlin, Ruth. *The Wind Leaves No Shadow.*
Momaday, M. Scott. *House Made of Dawn.*
Nichols, John. *The Magic Journey.*
Otis, Raymond. *Fire in the Night.* *
Richter, Conrad. *The Sea of Grass.*
Rhodes, Eugene Manlove. *Stepsons of Light.*
Waters, Frank. *The Man Who Killed the Deer.*

Non Fiction:

Austin, Mary. *The Land of Little Rain.* *
Ball, Eve. *Indeh.*
Calvin, Ross. *Sky Determines.* *
Cave, Dorothy. *Beyond Courage.* *
Chauvenet, Beatrice. *Hewett and Friends.*
Chavez, Fray Angélico. *My Penitente Land.* *
Clary, David. *Rocket Man.*
Cleaveland, Agnes M. *Satan's Paradise.* *
Crawford, Stanley. *The River in Winter.*
DeBuys, William and Harris, Alex. *River of Traps.*
Hordes, Stanley. *To The Ends of the Earth.*
Horgan, Paul. *Lamy of Santa Fe.*
Horgan, Paul. *The Centuries of Santa Fe.*
Keleher, William A. *The Fabulous Frontier.* *

King, Bruce. *Cowboy in the Roundhouse.* *
Kraft, Louis. *Gatewood and Geronimo.*
Kunetka, James. *City of Fire.*
La Farge, Oliver. *Behind the Mountains.* *
Larson, Robert. *New Mexico's Quest for Statehood.*
Lisle, Laurie. *Portrait of an Artist.*
McKenna, James. *Black Range Tales.*
Magoffin, Susan. *Down the Santa Fe Trail Into Mexico.*
Makeeta, Jaqueline. *Legacy of Honor.*
Marriott, Alice. *Maria The Potter of San Ildefonso.*
Mauldin, Bill. *A Sort of a Saga.*
Newcomb, Franc. *Hosteen Klah.*
Otero-Warren, Nina. *Old Spain in Our Southwest.* *
Pearson, Jim. *The Maxwell Land Grant.*
Robertson, Edna and Nestor, Sara. *Artists of the Canyons and Caminos.*
Sides, Hampton. *Blood and Thunder.*
Simmons, Marc. *Spanish Government in New Mexico.*
Sonnichsen, C.L. *Tularosa.*
Utley, Robert. *High Noon in Lincoln.*
Whaley, Charlotte. *Nina Otero Warren of Santa Fe.* *

*Published by Sunstone Press

Fifty-Plus Books on New Mexico from Sunstone Press

Agoyo, Herman, ed. *When Cultures Meet, Remembering the First Spanish Settlement in New Mexico.*

Austin, Mary. *The Land of Little Rain.*

Barco, Kathy. *READiscover New Mexico, A Tri-Lingual Adventure in Literacy.*

Cargo, David Francis. *Lonesome Dave, The Story of New Mexico Governor David Francis Cargo.*

Cave, Dorothy. *Beyond Courage.*

Cave, Dorothy. *Four Trails to Valor: From Ancient Footprints to Modern Battlefields, a Journey of Four Peoples.*

Chávez, Fray Angélico. *But Time and Chance: The Story of Padre Martinez of Taos, 1793–1867.*

De Aragón, Ray John. *The Penitentes of New Mexico.*

Ellis, Florence Hawley. *San Gabriel Del Yungue, the First Capital of New Mexico.*

Garrett, Pat F. *The Authentic Life of Billy the Kid.*

Hall, Ruth K. *A Place of Her Own: The Story of Elizabeth Garrett, the Daughter of Pat Garrett.*

Hertzog, Peter. *Outlaws of New Mexico.*

Holmes, Allan. *Fort Selden, 1865–1891.*

Keleher, William A. *The Fabulous Frontier, 1846–1912.*

Keleher, William A. *Maxwell Land Grant.*

Keleher, William A. *Memoirs, Episodes in New Mexico History, 1892 – 1969.*

Keleher, William A. *Turmoil in New Mexico, 1846–1868.*

Keleher, William A. *Violence in Lincoln County, 1869–1881.*

King, Bruce. *Cowboy in the Roundhouse.*

Lacy, Ann and Valley-Fox, Anne. *Frontier Stories.*

Lacy, Ann and Valley-Fox, Anne. *Lost Treasures and Old Mines.*

Lacy, Ann and Valley-Fox, Anne. *Outlaws and Desperados.*

Lavash, Donald R. *A Journey Through New Mexico History.*

McCord, Richard. *The Other State, New Mexico USA.*

McCulloch, Frank. *Revolution And Rebellion, How Taxes Cost a Governor His Life in 1830s New Mexico.*

McGeagh, Robert. *Juan De Onate's Colony in the Wilderness.*

Melzer, Richard. *Buried Treasures, Famous and Unusual Gravesites in New Mexico History.*

Melzer, Richard. *Ernie Pyle in the American Southwest.*

Nolan, Frederick. *The Life and Death of John Henry Tunstall.*

Nolan, Frederick. *The Lincoln County War.*

Otero, Miguel Antonio. *My Life On the Frontier, 1864–1882.*

Otero, Miguel Antonio. *My Life On the Frontier, 1882–1897.*

Otero, Miguel Antonio. *My Nine Years As Governor of the Territory of New Mexico, 1897–1906.*

Otero, Miguel Antonio. *The Real Billy the Kid.*

Otero-Warren, Nina. *Old Spain in Our Southwest.*

Poe, John William. *The Death of Billy the Kid.*

Prince, L. Bradford. *Historical Sketches of New Mexico.*

Prince, L. Bradford. *New Mexico's Struggle For Statehood.*

Prince, L. Bradford. *The Student's History of New Mexico.*

Reed, Benjamin. *An Illustrated History of New Mexico* (English and Spanish Editions).

Rickards, Colin. *Sheriff Pat Garrett's Last Days.*

Rogers, Everett M. and Bartlit, Nancy R. *Silent Voices of World War II, When Sons of the Land of Enchantment Met Sons of the Land of the Rising Sun.*

Silverman, Jason. *Untold New Mexico, Stories From a Hidden Past.*

Stanley, F. *The Grant that Maxwell Bought.*

Turk, David S. *Blackwater Draw: Three Lives, Billy the Kid and the Murders that Started the Lincoln County War.*

Twitchell, Ralph Emerson. *The Leading Facts of New Mexican History, Vol I.*

Twitchell, Ralph Emerson. *The Leading Facts of New Mexican History, Vol. II.*

Twitchell, Ralph Emerson. *The Military Occupation of the Territory of New Mexico, 1846–1851.*

Twitchell, Ralph Emerson. *Old Santa Fe.*

Twitchell, Ralph Emerson. *The Spanish Archives of New Mexico, Volume One.*

Twitchell, Ralph Emerson. *The Spanish Archives of New Mexico, Volume Two.*

Wallace, Susan. *The Land of the Pueblos.* Whaley, Charlotte. *Nina Otero-Warren of Santa Fe.*

Weigle, Marta. *Brothers of Light, Brothers of Blood: The Penitentes of the Southwest.*

www.ingramcontent.com/pod-product-compliance
Lightning Source LLC
Chambersburg PA
CBHW051715040426
42446CB00008B/898